POCKET IMAGES

Garsington

POCKET IMAGES

Garsington

Marion Gunther

NONSUCH

First published 1993
This new pocket edition 2007
Images unchanged from first edition

Nonsuch Publishing Limited
Cirencester Road, Chalford
Stroud, Gloucestershire, GL6 8PE
www.nonsuch-publishing.com

Nonsuch Publishing is an imprint of NPI Media Group

British Library Cataloguing in Publication Data.
A catalogue record for this book is available from the British Library.

ISBN 978-1-84588-417-8

Typesetting and origination by Nonsuch Publishing Limited
Printed in Great Britain

Contents

Introduction

The village of Garsington lies at the end of a horseshoe-shaped limestone ridge three miles southeast of Oxford. The buildings are clustered on the slopes of the ridge, which is 385 ft high. The underlying geological structure is interesting, with layers of stone and sand above the Oxford clay, and it accounts for numerous springs. These, and the brooks running from them, have given the village fields their names: Brook Furlong, Ellwell Field, Priestwell Field, Brockwell and Blindwell.

Garsington is mentioned in Domesday Book (1086), but its origins are probably much older. The Old English name—Gaersen dun, a grassy hill—describes the site, which has dramatic views in every direction: across the valley to Oxford, southwards to the Berkshire Downs and Wittenham Clumps, and eastwards to the Chilterns. A network of rights of way criss-crosses the hillside and one of these, the Roman Way, marks the western edge of the parish.

The varied topsoil consists of clay and loam, and the subsoil is a mixture of gravel and limestone. There is little true woodland, but the Oxford colleges which owned the land made plantations, and fine elm trees once bordered the fields. These provided a rich habitat for wildlife until Dutch elm disease destroyed most of these landmarks in the 1970s. Trees are planted annually to make good some of the loss, mainly with the help of grants allocated to the parish by Oxfordshire County Council.

Houses in Garsington were traditionally built of local limestone which was quarried from the hillside to the northwest of the village until the nineteenth century, when local bricks from the works in Kiln Lane also became available. The buildings of the medieval village were grouped at the top of the hill and around the Green, near to the church and the Manor House. Later the village grew to include the Old School (now converted into houses) and three pubs, the Plough Inn, the Red Lion and the Three Horseshoes. The village cross, which dates from 1240, survives, and the older houses dating from the sixteenth, seventeenth and eighteenth centuries have now been listed by the Department of the Environment. Some of these are fine timber-framed buildings, and medieval crucks have been found in two of the cottages. Ten thatched houses remain, but others were pulled down earlier this century and some have been re-roofed with tiles.

Agriculture has always been the main occupation of the villagers. Market gardening thrived on the loamy soils around the village and was encouraged by the six Oxford colleges which had estates there. The farming community is still very much alive, and most of the land is used for arable. In the past the village was home to a wide range of craftsmen and tradesmen, including blacksmiths, carpenters, shoemakers and wheelwrights. There was also a bakehouse and a butchers.

Since Morris Motors was set up in nearby Cowley in 1913, the pattern of life in the village has radically altered. In order to accommodate the growing number of workers from the car factory, new estates have been built at the lower end of the village around the Oxford Road. Many villagers are still employed at the plant, which is now owned by the Rover Group.

Today Garsington has a population of about 2,000 inhabitants. In spite of this growth and the changing pattern of work, many established families continue to live and work in the village. The names Clinkard, Druce, Durbridge, Parsler, Quainton, Townsend and Yeates, to name a few, will be familiar to many local people. Village activities still thrive, and the village hall and the Sports & Social Club cater for a wide variety of interests. The church and pubs provide lively social centres, and the primary school educates children from Garsington and Cuddesdon, and has a roll of nearly 200 pupils. The Garsington Players perform a play each summer in the famous gardens of the Manor House.

Many of the photographs in this book are from private collections and have not been published before. They show a variety of pastimes and reveal a different way of life, and they suggest a more tranquil world which people will look back on with nostalgia.

One

Old Buildings and Landmarks

Many old buildings remain in the village and form attractive groups, especially in the centre around the Green. Old buildings are also found in Southend and Pettiwell. Some of the cottages and farmhouses date from the seventeenth century, and a few, such as the Old Kennels and Library Farm, possibly from the sixteenth century. Library Farm, for instance, is mentioned in a 1636 lease of Exeter College, whose library benefited from the rent, and the building may be older. The local building materials were coursed rubblestone, brick, plaster and wattle-and-daub filling. Some houses are whitewashed and thatched, others have tiled roofs, and two are timber-framed. The Old Kennels and Library Farm, in Oxford Road, and Home Close in Southend, are fine examples of yeomen's farmhouses. In Pettiwell, once known as Salter's Lane, there is a particularly good collection of old buildings which is well worth a visit. Two of the three public houses, the Red Lion and the Three Horseshoes, date from the eighteenth century, a period of growth and rebuilding in the village.

Among the other notable sights in the village are the Cross, commonly known as the Stocks, with its medieval base, and the elegant First World War memorial. A sixteenth-century stone archway which marks the entrance to the original Rectory is still intact, and so is the brew house which lies to the north of the Manor House. The present Rectory dates from 1872. The Gizzel, with its ancient stone steps, is a spring-fed pond from which villagers used to draw water and gather watercress. In Pettiwell, between Lanesra Cottage and Pettiwell House, are old stone steps which lead to a kissing gate on an ancient right of way to the church, and a water pump still stands on the bank outside Pettiwell House. An eighteenth-century dovecote can be seen from Church Walk, a well-preserved building of mellow stone which stands on private land, and there is a staddle-stoned granary in the garden of Home Close.

The Cross in a painting by A.R. Quainton of 1919. A row of cottages dating from the seventeenth to eighteenth century stand back from the Green in the centre of the village.

The view looking towards Blenheim, a local name for part of the Wheatley Road. The cottage on the right, which was built in the seventeenth to eighteenth century, was the home of Mr Godfrey for many years. Opposite is the war memorial.

The war memorial, erected to the memory of village men who lost their lives in the First and Second World Wars. It is framed by two elm trees, with the Green in the background.

A view of the cluster of old houses in the alley leading from the war memorial to Oxford Road, c. 1920. The whitewashed bakehouse is just visible, and on the other side is a thatched cottage which has been tiled since this photograph was taken.

The village centre around 1940, showing the Old School wall with the magnificent beech tree. Opposite is part of the Green and in the foreground are Rectory Cottage and Glebe Cottage which date from the seventeenth to eighteenth century.

The Plough Inn, Pettiwell, a listed mid-eighteenth-century building. In 1842 it was bought by J.W. Clinch, founder of Witney Breweries, and in 1963 it was taken over by Courage Breweries.

Lanesra Cottage after conversion to a single dwelling, c. 1960.

The Thatched Cottage in Pettiwell, the home of the author, under several inches of snow in December 1961. The Durbridge family's six children grew up here. The building dates from the sixteenth to seventeenth century and is snug in its drystone-walled close.

Two sixteenth- to seventeenth-century houses in Pettiwell, c. 1890. Behind the wall is Pettiwell House, a fine timber-framed dwelling. In the background is Shepherd's Cottage which was renovated in 1972, when two scarf joints were discovered. The cottage is now tiled.

Pettiwell, Garsington.

A picturesque thatched cottage in Pettiwell (c. 1925), which was known then as Salter's Lane. The cottage was built in the sixteenth to seventeenth century, is timber framed and has the blade of a medieval cruck. The two Sellar sisters are sitting on the old stone steps which lead to an ancient footpath to the church.

GARSINGTON. 12

A group of attractive houses in Pettiwell, c. 1910–30. A drystone wall surrounds the Thatched Cottage which dates from the sixteenth to seventeenth century. There is an imposing view of Pettiwell House on the right, with Shepherd's Cottage behind and part of City Farm opposite.

Dovecote, Manor Farm House, c. 1920. The dovecote has a pyramidal roof, with ashlar nesting boxes inside, and it was constructed in the eighteenth century. The building is visible from Church Walk, an ancient footpath from Pettiwell to St Mary's church.

The Old Kennels, Oxford Road, c. 1890. This late seventeenth-century building has interesting ball-finials on the end of each gable. Around 1874 it became the home of James Clinkard, huntsman to Christ Church beagles. Kennels were built behind the house, and beagles were kept there until 1960.

The interior of the Old Kennels (c. 1890), showing a cosy front room with many standard Victorian trimmings.

The orchard at Library Farm, c. 1890. The house, set back in a dip from the Oxford Road, dates from the sixteenth century and has eighteenth-century additions. Mr S.W. King bought the farm from Exeter College in 1921.

A view of Oxford Road and the houses on the steep side of Clinkard's Hill, c. 1890.

Oxford Road looking towards Cowley in 1960. On the left a pavement has replaced the grass verge, and the houses here represent some of the modern infilling which has taken place in the village.

A view of Oxford Road looking towards the village. This sombre row of houses was built between the wars.

The Big Alley which criss-crosses down to the Little Alley and the Oxford Road, c. 1910. Some of the old cottages have been pulled down, and the alley is now part of The Hill.

Sadler's Croft, c. 1890. This old enclosure is named after the Sadler family who owned it in the eighteenth century.

A view of the Wheatley Road around 1940, looking towards Wheatley. The grass verges have since been replaced by pavements.

City Farm, c. 1890. These are the last buildings on the west side of Wheatley Road. The farm is part of the Oxford City Estate, and is also known as Surman's Farm. The farmhouse itself is in Pettiwell.

Hill Farm, c. 1890. This building dates from the seventeenth to eighteenth century and adjoins the yard of the Three Horseshoes public house. The names of the children are unknown.

A family outside the Three Horseshoes, c. 1890. The building dates from the eighteenth century and is set back from the Green. It has been a Morrells house since 1823.

An early seventeenth-century thatched cottage, pictured here on the right, c. 1868. This limestone rubble building stood on land which is now part of the new graveyard. The tree-lined road leads past the Gizzel and the Manor, and down the hill.

Home Close, Southend (c. 1910), which was formerly known as the Bailiff's House. The building stands well back from the road on a raised terrace, and is eighteenth century. During the First World War it was used as living quarters for friends of the Morrells who owned the Manor. More recently it was the home of the cartoonist Haro Hodson and his wife, writer Elisabeth Mavor.

The granary in the garden of Home Close, c. 1910. The building is raised on staddle stones to prevent vermin getting at the grain. It is timber framed, with a pyramidal roof. Aldous Huxley describes this granary in his novel Crome Yellow, calling the staddle stones 'toadstools'.

Attractive cottages in Southend, c. 1902. In the foreground is No. 41 which was occupied for many years by the Sellar family who were harness-makers. Next door is Midsummer Cottage which was thatched in those days and used as an alehouse; the roof is now tiled.

GARSINGTON. 16

A tranquil spot in Southend, c. 1920. The cottage in the foreground dates from the sixteenth to seventeenth century, and is timber-framed on a stone base. Around 1861 it was a pub known as the Seven Bells, the tenant being Richard Surman.

Another view of Seven Bells Cottage.

Southend Farmhouse, c. 1890. This sixteenth-century building has an eighteenth-century timber-framed wing. It is no longer a farm, but still belongs to Queen's College.

A view of Southend taken at the bottom of the hill, showing mid-twentieth-century development. Beyond the tree is the former Seven Bells pub.

Mid-twentieth-century houses in Southend, which replaced old cottages. The last of the surviving thatched cottages is just visible in front of the whitewashed house. The view looks away from the village towards Watlington Road.

Old Farmhouse in disrepair, c. 1907.

College Farm Barn, Southend, c. 1960. It has now been repaired and re-roofed.

Derelict barn with fine timbered roof, c. 1890. The exact situation of the barn is unknown and the building has probably completely disappeared.

An aerial view of Garsington, looking north, 1963. Since then most of the fine elm trees have been destroyed by Dutch elm disease. Part of Garsington Manor can be seen in the lower right hand corner, and St Mary's church is in the centre of the foreground. A path leads to the left from the church to Pettiwell and its group of cottages. The road past the Manor, on the right, is Southend, and the triangular Green is in the centre. From the Green, Oxford Road leads off to the top left and Wheatley Road branches to the right.

Two

Garsington Church

St Mary's church, on its hilltop site, is a landmark for many miles. From the porch and churchyard there are glorious views over the Thames Valley to Wittenham Clumps and the Berkshire Downs beyond. The simple, rather austere, outline of the building stands out against the gently undulating meadowland. Even on a wintry day, the memorial seat below the tower is a peaceful retreat.

The church is constructed of grey limestone, and the tower, which was built around 1200, is the oldest surviving part. The roof dates from the fifteenth century, as do the porch and some amusing gargoyles which were restored in the mid-nineteenth century. The clock was made by John Thwaites of Clerkenwell in 1796 and was a gift from the Harper family. It has faces on the north and south walls of the tower, and each dial has a single hand and is marked in quarter hours. In 1985 the clock was renovated and an automatic winder installed as a gift from the Caistor family in memory of their parents. The chancel is an early Decorated work (c. 1300), with simple geometrical tracery in the windows.

There are some notable eighteenth-century memorials in the church, including the Sadler memorial behind the door which commemorates three generations of that family. A more modern memorial by Eric Gill shows in shallow relief the profile of Lady Ottoline Morrell who died in 1938. In the tower there is a good peal of six inscribed bells. The beautiful stained-glass window at the east end of the church was placed there in 1898 by the late Frederick Parker Morrell in memory of his father.

The church was completely restored at a cost of £1,073 in 1849 when the building was re-roofed, the floor renewed and the chancel arch rebuilt. The money was raised within the parish by a subscription which was launched by the Revd James Ingram. During the renovations, the original stone altar was uncovered and installed in the chancel.

In the 1960s fêtes were held in the gardens of the Manor House in order to raise money for a new heating system for the church. When this was installed it was dedicated to the memory of Revd Anthony Pritchard. Fund-raising events have continued every year and in 1992, after years of hard work and organization, there was enough money to relay the chancel floor.

St Mary's church from the northwest, c. 1870. The building is a landmark for many miles around.

A fine view from the southeast of the church, taken in 1902 before most of the gravestones were removed. The surrounding wall is an ancient monument, and the porch dates from the fifteenth century.

The clock in the Norman tower, visible on both north and south faces, was made by John Thwaites in 1796. It has a single hand, is marked in quarter hours and it chimes hourly. The gate in the foreground leads to Church Walk, an ancient right of way.

The church interior, 1902. This view shows the nave looking towards the beautiful stained-glass east window above the altar, which was replaced in 1898.

An early twentieth-century view of the lych gate and churchyard surrounded by numerous elms, many of which have since died. The three prominent crosses mark the graves of the well-known Gale family. Joseph Gale, born in 1814, lived to be 98.

Church of St Mary from the northeast, c. 1902. In the foreground is the ivy-covered lych gate.

The lych gate, thought to be fifteenth century. The thatched cottage in the background is Stone House, which dates from the seventeenth century.

Parsonage House and dovecote, c. 1868. This Tudor house was deemed to be 'of no use' and was eventually pulled down. The house was a retreat for the scholars of Trinity College. In the 1860s Rider Haggard lived here for two years, and he describes the house in his autobiography.

The Old Rectory, a stately building, c. 1925. This Victorian house was built in 1872 for the rector, Revd D. Thomas. It is now a private house, and a smaller rectory has been built in the grounds.

Three

Garsington Manor

The Manor House is one of the most interesting houses in the county. It dates from the early sixteenth century, although its present appearance is largely the result of remodelling in the mid-seventeenth century. The building is of local grey rubblestone, and the elegant front door has an arched, leaded hood. The windows are symmetrically arranged and they have four-centred arches, and the roof is surmounted by a cupola. The house is set back from the road in a gravelled courtyard and flanked by two magnificent yew hedges, believed to be the highest in England. Eighteenth-century gateposts mark the entrance, and in the middle of the courtyard, clearly visible from the road, is a stone statue of a cherub on a pedestal holding a bunch of grapes.

The garden is formal, with sloping lawns, numerous yew hedges sheltering attractive flower borders, and a very old ilex tree. The lake and adjacent fishponds date back to monastic times. This fine garden was laid out by the Morrells in the 1920s, and has been developed since then. In the garden there is a well-preserved seventeenth-century dovecote, with wall recesses for nesting. The garden is open to the public twice a year as part of the National Garden Scheme.

In its present form the Manor dates from about 1625, when it was bought by William Wickham and extensively remodelled. As records show, there has been a manor house on the site since the thirteenth century when it was owned by the de Hauville family. It was bought by Thomas Chaucer in 1428. Over the next two hundred years the house changed hands frequently, until it was purchased by the Wickham family. It was then leased to Mr Quartermain and later to Mr Gale.

In 1914 Phillip Morrell and his wife Lady Ottoline bought the Manor, which was to become celebrated as a refuge for those of her friends who were conscientious objectors to the First World War, and as a meeting place for distinguished artists and intellectuals. Among the guests were Virginia Woolf, Mark Gertler, Aldous Huxley, D.H. Lawrence, John Maynard Keynes, Bertrand Russell and many more of the Bloomsbury Group.

More recent owners have been the Oxford don Dr Heaton, followed by the well-known historian Sir John Wheeler-Bennett and his wife Lady Ruth. Sir John resided there until his death in 1975. The present owners are Mr and Mrs Leonard Ingram who have begun a programme of musical performances and an opera season, which is becoming well known. This idyllic setting is also used by the Garsington Players for their summer productions.

One of Garsington's original manor houses, shown in an old, undated engraving. This may be Louches Manor House of Northend, which is now the site of North Manor Estate.

Garsington Manor House. This photograph, which shows the Manor in its present form, was taken in the 1860s from the southwest.

The Manor House in the 1930s.

10. Manor House. Garsington

The front of the Manor House, c. 1930. The house is flanked by yew hedges which are reputed to be the highest in England.

A view across the courtyard, taken from the main entrance. Particular features of note are the elegant arched hood over the door, the gabled attics and the central tiled cupola.

The dovecote in the grounds of Garsington Manor, c. 1920. The inscription above the door dates it to 1714. It has a steep tiled roof and a lantern, and there are nesting places inside.

A garden party at Garsington Manor. As this picture dates from before the First World War, the party may have been held to celebrate the coronation of Edward VII in 1902 or George V in 1911.

Fête, in aid of church funds, held in the garden of the Manor in June 1962. The picture is taken from across the lake and shows the terraced lawns and the west face of the house beyond. The Italianate garden was created by Lady Ottoline Morrell in the 1920s.

People waiting to go boating on the lake during the fête held at the Manor in 1962.

Four

The Village School

The school was built in 1840 for 110 children of the village on what was then the Green. It is constructed of local grey limestone and the style is Tudor Gothic. The imposing building is a landmark in the centre of the village, at the highest point of the hill. The Green was leased to Trinity College for 999 years in 1839 on condition that a school and house be provided for the master. This arrangement was doubly pleasing to the Revd James Ingram, then president of Trinity College and rector of Garsington, because the school and house encroached on the Green, stopping the villagers from using it for Sunday cricket and bull-baiting. Two classrooms were provided, one on either side of the master's house, with a bell tower in the centre of the roof. The bell rope hung down into the kitchen so the children could be summoned conveniently to the school. In 1886 a further classroom was added to the south of the building to accommodate the increasing number of pupils.

In 1984 the school moved to a new building off Wheatley Road which takes approximately 200 children from Garsington and nearby Cuddesdon. The Old School has now been converted into three luxury houses.

Garsington school, c. 1875. This photograph shows the school in its original form of a classroom on either side of the master's house. It was built in 1840.

The school, showing the additional classroom added in 1886.

The new classroom. This close-up shows the extension to the school which provided the extra space needed to accommodate the growing number of village children.

The school interior in 1905, showing the partition of glass and wood which was added to segregate the third classroom from the others.

May Day procession of schoolchildren, taken in Pettiwell in the 1890s during Mr Muscott's headmastership.

Mr Muscott's junior class in the playground at the turn of the century.

The school, 1904. This picture of the front of the Tudor Gothic building clearly shows its construction of local limestone with quoins of Bath and Box stone.

A view of the village school from the junction with Oxford Road, 1905. In the foreground is the hedge around the village hall.

Undivided attention: a picture of a class and teacher taken in 1905 during Mr Muscott's headmastership. The glass and wood divider is clearly visible.

A mixed class in the school playground in 1916, shortly after the arrival of the new headmaster, Mr S.G. Gidney (with moustache). The late Fred Pym is holding the board. Note the neatness and simplicity of dress.

Assembly: the infant class stands to greet the arrival of their teacher. This charming picture was taken on 7 November 1905.

School class, c. 1907.

A serious-looking class photographed by the main door, c. 1910. Family likenesses are apparent among these children who were probably from the middle school.

Infant class in the school playground (c. 1928), showing two of Mr Gidney's assistant teachers, Miss Higgs and Avis Clarke. Many of these pupils are present-day pensioners who are possibly still recognizable, and among them are children with familiar village names like Clinkard, Druce, Wheeler and Yeates.

Girls' cookery class in the 1930s. These two pictures were taken at the Rectory Barn Room, a location that provided scope for their skills away from the classroom. The boys were sent to the old Wheatley primary school hut for woodwork.

Cricket XI, 1933. The school team contains boys from Miss Butler's middle class, and they are photographed in the playground, with the greenhouse in the background. Boys were taught the art of gardening as part of the school curriculum.

Mr S.G. Gidney, headmaster 1915–52, with colleagues in the front garden of the school house at a social gathering after the Second World War.

Mrs Elsie Caistor and her staff with 5 to 11 year olds, c. 1956.

Mrs Money, a primary school teacher, with her infant class, 1962. The copse in the background is in the grounds of Manor Farm House and is known as The Plantation.

May Day celebrations in the Old School playground, 1970. The children dancing around the maypole are being watched by a large gathering of parents and villagers. Mr M. Royal was then headmaster.

Last day of the Old School, 18 February 1984. This valedictory picture was taken when Garsington primary school was closed. It shows Mr Harold Shepherd, aged 87, the oldest living former pupil, with the present-day children, who are suitably attired. The new school had just been opened in Wheatley Road.

Five

Work and Leisure

During the nineteenth and early twentieth centuries, most people in the village worked on the land, employed by farmers, market gardeners and agricultural engineers. A flourishing brickworks in Kiln Lane provided work for others. Shoemakers and harness-makers, carpenters, blacksmiths and wheelwrights thrived in the village, as did the butcher, the baker, the general store and the post office in the village centre. The pattern of working life in the village changed when Morris Motors and Pressed Steel were set up at nearby Cowley; these works absorbed much of the village's labour force as well as attracting new residents.

Recreational activities centred around the village hall, the Rectory Barn Room and the three public houses. Most national organizations were represented. For young people there were the Boy Scouts, the Girl Guides, a boys' club and the Girls' Friendly Society. For the adults there were the Mothers' Union, the Women's Institute, Toc H, the British Legion, a village dramatic society and football and cricket clubs. Games such as cribbage, shove-halfpenny and Aunt Sally were played in the pubs. Whist drives and dances were held in the village hall and the church was supported by a strong choir. The annual two-day feast on the Green was a highlight, particularly enjoyed by the younger people.

Baker's boy: an enchanting photograph of Fred Durbridge, aged 6, at a fancy dress party held in the village hall in 1929.

Farmworkers busy haymaking in a field behind Library Farm. The elm trees were landmarks before they were destroyed by Dutch elm disease. Ancient rights of way lead from here to Kiln Lane and Salter's Lane (now Pettiwell).

Carting timber, a familiar scene in the village in the late nineteenth century.

Harvesting Brownleys Fields, on Capt. Woodruffe's land, 1910. An extra horse is being used to pull the two-horse binding machine.

Farmworkers in Manor Farm House yard, c. 1910. Manor Farm then belonged to Capt. Woodruffe.

A typical haymaking scene during the 1890s, when men, women and children helped with the harvesting.

A haymaking group taking a break, c. 1890.

Mr 'Willum' Woodwards, c. 1910. Woodwards, who was carter to Capt. Woodruffe for many years, is pictured leading the stallion Prince in the yard of Manor Farm House.

Market gardening: Mr Hugo Druce planting cabbages in the spring of 1962. The land adjoins Church Walk, and a right of way follows the line of the elm trees which were later destroyed by disease.

A tea party held in the Old Rectory garden, c. 1890. Three smart maids take a break outside the marquee.

Mr William John Eden, the local policeman, 1904. He lived in the Police House, a thatched cottage next door to the Old Bakery in Oxford Road. This cottage has since burnt down. His mere presence was enough to keep law and order!

Mr E. Druce and his dog Tootser in the 1920s. He is drawing water from a tap in the wall which served villagers living nearby in Wheatley Road and The Hill.

The band of the Benefits Society with village men in 1885. The present society is called the Ancient Order of Foresters.

Children on the swings at the Garsington village feast, c. 1890. This annual fair was held on the Green in the centre of the village until the 1960s.

Children's parade, near the Old Bakehouse, on Clinkard's Hill, c. 1890.

Queen Victoria's Diamond Jubilee celebrations, 1897. A group of villagers, old and young, enjoy a day off on this unique occasion, and pose for the photographer Joseph Turrill in front of the school.

The interior of the Red Lion public house, where a sumptuous feast has been laid out to celebrate the Diamond Jubilee.

Villagers parade to celebrate the Diamond Jubilee. The school bell tower is visible in the background.

The Diamond Jubilee celebrations committee, photographed opposite the Plough Inn, with the school and garden in the background. Mr Muscott, the headmaster of the school, and his wife are seated in the second row on the right. Some of the villagers in the picture bear familiar family names, including Blay, Clinkard, Druce, Parsler, Surman and Yeates.

The Boys Brigade and their band celebrating the coronation of King Edward VII in 1902.

Mothers and children: a picture taken to commemorate the coronation of King Edward VII.

Mr Cherry John Tom Smith led the pageant on a donkey when the village celebrated Queen Elizabeth II's coronation in 1953. The procession is on the Green, outside the school.

Pageant, 1953. This picture, taken in the school playground, shows Mr Cherry John Tom Smith on his decorated donkey with a group of village children.

A British Legion group opposite the Plough Inn (c. 1935), on the occasion of a rally held at Hatfield. The school is in the background. The men in the group include: Dr Heaton, Capt. Woodruffe, Mr Witcombe, Herbie Clinkard, Lionel Quainton, Percy Sawyer, Jack Reid, Mr J. Jennings, Bert Durbridge, Sammy Wheeler, Jock Simpkins, Jack Maule.

The Home Guard in the early 1940s. Seated in the centre at the front are the two officers, Capt. J. Jennings and Lt. Lowensky.

Nigel Gidney, the eldest son of Mr S.G. Gidney, in RAF uniform in 1938. He is standing with his brother in the garden of the school house.

Special Constable S.G. Gidney, 1940. Mr Gidney, the school headmaster, is shown studying his orders at the front door of the school house before going on duty as a sergeant in the Special Constabulary.

British Legion party in the village hall, c. 1947. The party was given for the elderly residents of the village, with the help of the Women's Institute.

The Armistice Day service of 1961. The parade of the women's branch of the British Legion pauses at the war memorial.

Mothers' Union group outside the Old Rectory, c. 1930. The Reverend and Mrs Windley are sitting in the centre; he was the incumbent from 1928 to 1936.

Mothers' Union group in the Rectory garden on a warm summer's day in the 1950s.

The Garsington Cubs in the Rectory fields where they used to pitch their camp, c. 1935. Sitting in the centre, surrounded by her young charges, is Winifred Clinkard, Akela or cub leader.

Captain Woodruffe and his stallion in the yard of Manor Farm House, c. 1910. His field spaniel stands patiently in front of the old tiled barn.

An elegant picture of Mr and Mrs Blay leaving the yard of their home, Hill Farm, by horse and carriage during the 1920s. This old farmhouse faces the war memorial.

Dr McCausland doing his rounds on horseback at the turn of the century. Garsington was one of the villages which he most ably served.

Christ Church beagles on the land belonging to the Old Kennels at around the turn of the century.

Village men going on an outing in a two-horse brake, c. 1890.

The village cricket team on the cricket field in Salter's Lane, now known as Pettiwell, c. 1890.

Ladies playing tennis on the court at Clinkard's Farm in a charming picture taken at the end of the nineteenth century.

A village man proudly showing off his penny-farthing bicycle, late nineteenth century.

A cyclist with a penny-farthing chatting to a barmaid outside the Red Lion public house. The photograph was taken by Joseph Turrill around 1890.

Joseph Turrill in the 1890s. He lived at Fern Cottage and was a market gardener as well as a photographer. A fine collection of his photographs came to light in the 1960s and has been passed to the Oxfordshire Photographic Archive.

The Turrill sisters outside the Old Kennels, c. 1890. Two of them are sitting on the mounting stones.

Dressed for tennis: two photographs of the Turrill sisters Hettie and Lynne with friends in the garden of Fern Cottage, c. 1890.

Mixed doubles: a tennis group including the Turrill sisters on the court in the grounds of Clinkard's Farm, c. 1890.

One of the Turrill daughters with her cat in the sitting room of Fern Cottage, c. 1890.

Three village children, taken at the turn of the century.

Family group, 1910. This rather solemn photograph of Frederick Herbert Durbridge with his wife and children was taken in the large garden behind his home, The Mount, in Wheatley Road.

Wedding photograph taken by Joseph Turrill, c. 1890. The bride is Ethel E. Mary Young.

Family group at the wedding of Ethel E. Mary Young at Garden View Cottage, The Hill.

Wedding photograph, taken by Joseph Turrill, of Alice and Will Young. The high wall is part of Garden View Cottage, The Hill.

A delightful picture of the infant daughters of Alice and Will Young.

A beautiful photograph of Ethel Manning taken by Joseph Turrill on a special occasion in the early part of this century.

A wedding group photographed in 1910 in the garden of the Seven Bells public house in Southend at the marriage of Arthur Jacobs to Lizzie Godfrey.

Family group at the wedding of Edith and Fred Godfrey at the turn of the century.

Mr and Mrs John Godfrey at their wedding on Trafalgar Day, 21 October 1911.

Fifty years on: Rose and John (Jack) Godfrey on the occasion of their Golden Wedding in 1961. They are standing outside their cottage opposite the war memorial with their dog Lulu.

A lad with his new bicycle, photographed by Joseph Turrill in Pettiwell in the 1890s.

Acknowledgements

I would like to thank the many people who have helped and encouraged me to write this book, especially Mr David Brown. I am also very grateful to everyone who lent photographs and told me such fascinating stories about them, including: Mr and Mrs L. Bonner, Mr and Mrs H. Druce, Mr F. Durbridge, Mrs A. Eden, Mr and Mrs W. Eden, Mr P. Gidney, Mr Joe Jennings, Mr A. Parsler, Mr and Mrs V. Ruffels and Mr A.J. Smith. My special thanks also go to Nancy Hood and Nuala la Vertue for their help and support.

The publisher regrets that the reference made on the back cover to the butcher and baker is incorrect. Both tradesmen have long since been replaced, as village residents will no doubt know, by the general store and post office.

Sources

Garsington Local History Group, Garsington: A Brief Guide, 1987.
Garsington Women's Institute, Garsington, 1937.
Oxfordshire County Council Leisure & Arts, Central Library, Westgate, Oxford.
Oxfordshire Photographic Archive.
The Victoria History of the County of Oxford, Vol. 5: Bullingdon Hundred, 1957.